Paper Mountains

Paper Mountains

2020
Seabeck Haiku Getaway
Anthology

Tanya McDonald
Kelly Sauvage
editors

Haiku Northwest Press

Haiku Northwest Press
Bellevue, Washington

ISBN 978-1-953092-03-8

Copyright © 2021 by Haiku Northwest

All rights revert to the authors upon publication of this book. No part of this book may be used or reproduced in any manner whatsoever without written permission from the contributor, except in the case of brief quotations in reviews.

This anthology commemorates Haiku Northwest's 13th annual Seabeck Haiku Getaway, October 30–November 1, 2020, held online (via Zoom) due to the COVID-19 pandemic. All attendees who submitted to the anthology were guaranteed to have one poem published.

Layout by Tanya McDonald
Cover design and editorial advice by Michael Dylan Welch

www.haikunorthwest.org

Contents

In Each Other's Company 7

Haiku & Senryu 11

Kukai Winners 67

Index of Poets 75

In Each Other's Company

On an afternoon in mid-July 2020, Michael Dylan Welch and I sat outside at my house, safely distanced from each other due to the ongoing pandemic. During our four-hour conversation, we shifted from sun to shade and discussed the likelihood of being able to hold the thirteenth annual Seabeck Haiku Getaway in person. In the end, we decided that even if the Seabeck Conference Center were to be open for guests, we could not ask folks to put their health at risk by attending. And so, with a mixture of disappointment and excitement, brainstorming began for a virtual Seabeck getaway on the audio/video communications platform, Zoom.

One of the challenges we faced was how to retain the warm spirit and camaraderie of in-person Seabeck. Another was how to incorporate what have become Seabeck traditions over the years, such as the kukai (a traditional haiku contest) and sharing handmade haiku handouts. And as the number of registered attendees grew, it became clear that we would have to adapt certain activities for a larger group. For example, having everyone introduce themselves and share a haiku with the whole group would have taken more than two hours.

In the following months, Michael assembled an international assortment of speakers, readers, and facilitators, working his magic to create a bountiful schedule. This year's theme was "vision" and many of the presentations would reflect and explore that topic.

And so, on the weekend of October 30 to November 1, 2020, more than 200 people from fourteen different countries gathered for the first virtual Seabeck Haiku Getaway on Zoom. Around a quarter of the folks had attended a previous getaway, but for everyone else, this was their first taste of Seabeck. Due to geographic distances, many people might not have been able to attend in person, so that was certainly a silver lining to having Seabeck online. The getaway kicked off on Friday night with an open reading time where attendees could share their haiku and socialize. The next morning, Michael welcomed everyone with a slideshow of his Seabeck photos, taken over the past twelve years. It provided a much-needed sense of place for our gathering, for although folks were logging in from around the world, through Michael's photos we could all imagine that we were at Seabeck in Washington state, enjoying the view of the Olympic Mountains across Hood Canal, exploring the woods and lagoon, and hanging out in person.

Over the course of the weekend, we enjoyed varied readings and visual presentations of art. To accommodate socializing among such a large group, we made use of Zoom's breakout rooms, gathering in intimate numbers to share haiku, meet new folks, and reconnect with old friends. We found writing inspiration in the form of "Write Now" exercises and other workshops. Insightful presentations and lively discussions enriched our knowledge of haiku and its community. Since Saturday was Halloween, we invited folks to wear silly hats for a day's-end celebration, and Michael's squid hat inspired more than a few senryu. On Sunday evening, to continue one of our long-standing traditions, we encouraged submissions to the annual kukai. Participants voted on their favorite haiku and senryu through an online voting form, and Michael compiled the winning poems, which appear at the end of this anthology.

Everyone who attended Seabeck 2020 was invited to submit up to five haiku/senryu to the anthology, from which Kelly Sauvage and I selected one poem per person. Many of the poems reflect the weekend's events, from featured guest Tom Painting's workshop on bird haiku, to Brad Bennett's talk on euphony, to Yvette Kolodji's presentation on haiku inspired by science videos, to David Berger's presentation about the life and art of Fumiko Kimura. Other topics include the peculiarities of Zoom, and life during the pandemic. These 130 poems, along with the fifteen kukai winners, commemorate how, despite our physical distances, we came together out of a love of haiku and celebrated the best and oldest Seabeck tradition, spending time in each other's company. Enjoy the anthology!

Tanya McDonald

Haiku & Senryu

Seabeck 2020
a patchwork quilt
of friendly faces

Carol Judkins
Carlsbad, California

flossing only
my front teeth
Zoom meeting

Annette Makino
Arcata, California

moonlit screen
we gather to write
the silence

    Ron C. Moss
    Tasmania, Australia

within mere syllables expanding universe

    Terran Campbell
    Kirkland, Washington

red tailed hawk
I learn a new word
. . . enso . . .

    Mimi Ahern
    San Jose, California

the air
within and without you
bamboo flute

> *Scott Wiggerman*
> *Albuquerque, New Mexico*

dandelion
the thunder
of a hundred seeds

> *Anette Chaney*
> *Harrison, Arkansas*

deep breaths . . .
looking up
into the gold of willows

    Kathleen I. Tice
    Kent, Washington

candy colours
a leaf   leaves
its sugars in the tree

    Alice Wanderer
    Frankston, Australia

Santa Anna winds—
on the vine
stewed tomatoes

Seretta Martin
San Diego, California

hot zone . . .
between the sheets,
subduction

Henry Brann
Philadelphia, Pennsylvania

leaning into
the lava flow
pixelated ashes

Sari Grandstaff
Saugerties, New York

our extinction
hidden within the lake
my small poem

> *Dianne Garcia*
> *Seattle, Washington*

missing apostrophe
everything that isn't mine
to take

> *Jennifer Hambrick*
> *Columbus, Ohio*

after their words
digging deep
into pumpkin guts

> *Genevieve Wynand*
> *Coquitlam, British Columbia*

history textbook
covered
with old news

> *Baisali Chatterjee Dutt*
> *Kolkata, India*

under my shoe
on the shelf
a golden ginkgo leaf

> *Franci Louann*
> *New Westminster, British Columbia*

autumn
the euphony of rustling
poems

    Jonathan Roman
    Yonkers, New York

gurgling stream
listening to the sounds
of every word

    Christine Wenk-Harrison
    Lago Vista, Texas

last light
black ducks forage
for acorns

    Kristen Lindquist
    Camden, Maine

a thousand
snow geese in one photo
the Buson Challenge

    John S Green
    Bellingham, Washington

writer's block
my pen teasing
a paper hole

    Michelle Schaefer
    Bothell, Washington

crisscrossing
in sky-blue ether
autumn jet streams

    Victor Fleming
    Little Rock, Arkansas

Seabeck horizon
mistaking mountains
for clouds

    Lynne Jambor
    Vancouver, British Columbia

casting shadows
the fog
tells its own story

    Mike Rehling
    Presque Isle, Michigan

mockingbird—
I hold back
my narrative

    Hifsa Ashraf
    Rawalpindi, Pakistan

old bookmark . . .
searching for the word
where my mother stopped

    Lew Watts
    Chicago, Illinois

dark garden—
the rustle of something
not seen

    C. R. Manley
    Bellevue, Washington

through the blinds
watching my neighbour tango
alone

    Terry Ann Carter
    Victoria, British Columbia

last night's raindrops
catching dawn
on the windowpane

Lisa Gerlits
Silverton, Oregon

lunar nectar
my wish for a sip
of moon water

Kath Abela Wilson
Pasadena, California

high noon
standing ankle-deep
in my shadow

Firdaus Parvez
Aligarh, India

the lilies tall
and still
grandmother's gravesite

Charlotte Hrenchuk
Whitehorse, Yukon Territory

damp cenotaph~
        a poppy pinned
to the nearby sapling

Michael Dudley
Stratford, Ontario

Buddhist retreat . . .
not a bodhi tree in sight
free of statue

Kala Ramesh
Chennai, India

limestone quarry
two ravens
barricade the road

isabella mori
Richmond, British Columbia

second lockdown
all the balconies
empty

Roberta Beary
County Mayo, Ireland

breaking curfew
the moon out all night
again

    Marisa Fazio
    Melbourne, Australia

shadows that weren't
written there this morning . . .
insomnia

    Marita Gargiulo
    Hamden, Connecticut

drinking my coffee
I count the sheep
on her scarf

Priscilla Cook
Washington

wearing a mask
for a different reason
Halloween

Laura Quindt
Woodinville, Washington

Seabeck 20/20
a varied thrush
in my mind's eye

Tom Painting
Atlanta, Georgia

Seabeck Stayaway
zooms around the world
across the miles—smiles

> *Diane Wallihan*
> *Port Townsend, Washington*

Star Zoom
Tanya beams me
from room to room

> *Helen Ogden*
> *Pacific Grove, California*

zoom laughter . . .
on mute
the dog's snore

> *Madhuri Pillai*
> *Melbourne, Australia*

zoom gathering . . .
feeling naked
without my mask

Carole MacRury
Point Roberts, Washington

such embarrassment
discovering the mic
is still live

Vera Constantineau
Copper Cliff, Ontario

the lightness
of laughter
halloween hats

    Carole Harrison
    Jamberoo, Australia

hat parade
the squid
reigns supreme

    Patricia Wakimoto
    Gardena, California

squid birth
an undulating sea
of silly hats

Kat Lehmann
Guilford, Connecticut

halloween
ghosts of basho
exit meeting

John Budan
Newberg, Oregon

twilight fog
hanging in the air
your unanswered question

Ce Rosenow
Eugene, Oregon

autumn evening
I step into
the owl's dream

Jacob Salzer
Vancouver, Washington

spider season
flagging cedars settle
the year's accounts

R. J. Swanson
Rollingbay, Washington

fall camping
the damp wood
hisses and steams

David Berger
Seattle, Washington

the ants hurry home
dragging a dead lizard—
onset of winter

Lakshmi Iyer
Trivandrum, India

later the night
the mark of dog's bite
on my hand

Gurpreet Dutt
Srinagar, India

conspiracy theories—
so many termites
under the house

    Robin Palley
    Philadelphia, Pennsylvania

tectonic forces—
custody fight over
the schnauzer

    Alan Harvey
    Tacoma, Washington

fireworks
pop pop popping
painkillers

Julie Bloss Kelsey
Germantown, Maryland

the cardinal gets
his dark plumage early
summer depression

Susan Burch
Hagerstown, Maryland

thunder~
the dragon trumpets shake
and sway in the wind

Janis Albright Lukstein
Rancho Palos Verdes, California

zigzag hummingbirds
the circular rhythm
of razor wire

    Lorraine A. Padden
    San Diego, California

Above the beach
a path carves through yellow blooms
close to the ground

    MJ Newcomer
    Beaumont, California

moonless night
bioluminous water sprays
on a boat's wake

    Bona M. Santos
    Los Angeles, California

end of heavy rain—
stringing the outer rim
a spider starts over

Richard Tice
Kent, Washington

the wrinkles on my hand
autumn
web of life

Cathy Tashiro
Tacoma, Washington

what is your name?
missing rhinestones
in her favorite brooch

Dorothy Mahoney
Windsor, Ontario

narrowing trickle
the icy stream still
sparkles at sunrise

Sharon Young
Tok, Alaska

mini waterfall
through the beaver dam
her dementia worse

Pearl Pirie
Alcove, Quebec

winter dawn
already the moon
one quarter erased

June Rose Dowis
Shreveport, Louisiana

the year's first snow
if only
it would not be your last

Michael Dylan Welch
Sammamish, Washington

starless night
the wind lifts flakes of ash
from the dying fire

    Meredith Ackroyd
    Afton, Virginia

the sensei's life
crossing in and through
spots of light

    Dorothy Avery Matthews
    Poulsbo, Washington

her sumi brush skips
over fresh rice paper—
maples in the mist

    Wendy Toth Notarnicola
    Long Valley, New Jersey

painting class . . .
Fibonacci's signature
on a sunflower

Milan Rajkumar
Imphal, India

a father
chasing a child
chasing a butterfly

Garry Wilson
Issaquah, Washington

Bansuri raga
the embroidery
of birdsong

    Mary Stevens
    Hurley, New York

prima ballerina
her blushing cheeks
the color of her tutu

    Joan C. Fingon
    Ventura, California

lavender to red
deepening the brush strokes
of my words

    Claire Vogel Camargo
    Austin, Texas

Summer drizzle—
poking out of the mist,
purple thistle.

    Daphne Clifton
    Portland, Oregon

lingering heat
the cows below the meadow
deep in duckweed

    Bill Deegan
    Mahwah, New Jersey

the cooee
of an Eastern Koel
wet clover

Myron Lysenko
Woodend, Australia

sunny break . . .
an ant in the cup
of a crocus

Susan Constable
Parksville, British Columbia

watercolor brush
opens lotus blossom
spring rain

Sharon Lynne Yee
Torrance, California

first warm day
a new turtle
on the old log

> *Robert Forsythe*
> *Annandale, Virginia*

wildflowers
under the picnic rug
black ants

> *Bisshie*
> *Zürich, Switzerland*

dockyard—
briefly on a lamp standard
the eagle besieged by crows

    Vicki McCullough
    Vancouver, British Columbia

home again
her favorite bird
scolding me

    Sarah Metzler
    Marion Center, Pennsylvania

in the old neighbourhood
missing house
sparrows

kjmunro
Whitehorse, Yukon Territory

daybreak
shell fragments line
the empty nest

Michael Henry Lee
Saint Augustine, Florida

swirling wind . . .
curls
of last year's bark

Leanne Mumford
Sydney, Australia

medical leave
a layer of dust
on the desk

    Deborah P Kolodji
    Temple City, California

home schooling done now—
worn corners
of the wooden stool

    Mike Freiling
    Vancouver, Washington

new wrinkles
in the faces of friends
this autumn

    Bob Redmond
    Burien, Washington

hummingbirds
on the nasturtium remnants
do they know it's fall?

> *Aleksandra Monk*
> *Seattle, Washington*

high in the tree
red apples in my hands
as the ladder leans

> *Shirley Marc*
> *Springfield, Oregon*

All Hallow's Eve—
at till number six
a unicorn bags my groceries

elehna de sousa
Salt Spring Island, British Columbia

late October
shorter days burning
at both ends

Cynthia Anderson
Yucca Valley, California

Fall time change
calling home for permission
to dance another hour

> *Connie Hutchison*
> *Kirkland, Washington*

late autumn sun
my attention span
grows longer

> *Chandra Bales*
> *Albuquerque, New Mexico*

sumi-e
I follow the path
of the brush

> *Marion Clarke*
> *Warrenpoint, Northern Ireland*

a canyon walk
through light and shadows
our last Mother's Day

    Claudia Poquoc
    San Diego, California

looking down
at us looking up—
owlets

    Sheila Sondik
    Bellingham, Washington

a half-moon
on the baby's fingernail—
my whole world

    Terri L. French
    wherever the RV is

daughter turning my sunshine into woman

m. shane pruett
Salem, Oregon

grandma's house
November sun fills
the chestnut tree

Sarah Paris
Santa Rosa, California

sled crash . . .
kids' laughter flies
every which way

    Judt Shrode
    Tacoma, Washington

mother's button tin
my daughter learning to count
on my memories

    susan spooner
    Victoria, British Columbia

Seven hats on a rack
who can account for that or
this wild iris flowering

> *Noreen Lawlor*
> *Joshua Tree, California*

little actions
how tenderly the ant
touches an aphid

> *Shelley Baker-Gard*
> *Portland, Oregon*

a love song
two flickers
on the electrical line

> *Carmen Sterba*
> *University Place, Washington*

repairman—
remembering my mask
forgetting my bra

    Tanya McDonald
    Woodinville, Washington

zoom gala
black tie and
pyjama bottoms

    Maxianne Berger
    Outremont, Quebec

hot date
grand finale
lava cake

    Kim Weers
    Woodinville, Washington

hunter's blue moon
again
he proposes

Marilyn Powell
Morristown, New Jersey

mating season—
the sparrow lands
on a song

Pippa Phillips
St. Louis, Missouri

beneath a blanket of stars
the heat . . .
of your touch

    Cheryl Berrong
    Fairbanks, Alaska

standing on the rim of the volcano
my sense of self
just a trick of the mind

    Claudia Coutu Radmore
    Carleton Place, Ontario

ending the night
with an apology . . .
a robin's song

Christine L. Villa
North Highlands, California

just dawn—
indigo blooming
on your skin

Kashiana Singh
Chicago, Illinois

liminal the space between the loves-me bones

Kelly Sauvage
Madison, Wisconsin

finally starting
to live my dream
a blackbird's shadow

Angela Terry
Sequim, Washington

sumi-e
humming to herself
a song from home

Antoinette Cheung
Vancouver, British Columbia

snowflakes
soft on the grass
sashiko stitches

Sandra St-Laurent
Yukon Territory

flickers in streetlight
the globe of this nightworld
fills with snow

>   *Josephine LoRe*
>   *Calgary, Alberta*

the highway
empty and alone
a forward thrust

>   *Joan Marie Roberts*
>   *Victoria, British Columbia*

the time it takes
my mind to descend . . .
washi paper mountains

sidney bending
Victoria, British Columbia

an oak leaf
cartwheels down the street
lockdown lifts

Marilyn Ashbaugh
Edwardsburg, Michigan

Seabeck next year
we'll meet in person
hugs at long last

> *Emily W Kane*
> *Edmonds, Washington*

Kukai Winners

First Place

> dahlia blossom—
> the many layers
> of her touch
>
> *Nicholas Klacsanzky*
> *Seattle, Washington*

Second Place

dense fog
the murmuring
of our condolences

Lorraine A. Padden
San Diego, California

Third Place

vinegar & newspaper
wiping the windows
with stories

Dorothy Mahoney
Windsor, Ontario

Fourth Place

> rainforest
> we travel towards the mountains
> by flute
>
> *Marion Clarke*
> *Warrenpoint, Northern Ireland*

Fifth Place

dusting for fingerprints the whorl of galaxies

> *Sarah Metzler*
> *Marion Center, Pennsylvania*

Sixth Place (tie)

under the pile
of newly raked leaves—
giggles

> *Kim Weers*
> *Woodinville, Washington*

sumi brush
with one sweep
a leaf

> *Sarah Metzler*
> *Marion Center, Pennsylvania*

old bus ticket
between the pages
marking her stop

> *susan spooner*
> *Victoria, British Columbia*

Seventh Place

> letter to old friend
> returned to sender
> late autumn chill
>
> *Maureen Lanagan Haggerty*
> *Madison, New Jersey*

Eighth Place

> getting old
> the roots move around
> the stones
>
> *Mike Rehling*
> *Presque Isle, Michigan*

Ninth Place (tie)

fall colors
my choices of words
keep changing

> Christine L. Villa
> North Highlands, California

through a train window
the hunter's moon
stalking me

> Pippa Phillips
> St. Louis, Missouri

Tenth Place (tie)

    post mastectomy
        through her garden window
            two ripe tomatoes

Robin Palley
Philadelphia, Pennsylvania

Halloween moon
the disembodied voices
of passing geese

Jacquie Pearce
Vancouver, British Columbia

blue moon . . .
the fading notes
of a flute

Susan Constable
Parksville, British Columbia

Index of Poets

Ackroyd, Meredith 42
Ahern, Mimi 14
Anderson, Cynthia 52
Ashbaugh, Marilyn 64
Ashraf, Hifsa 23
Baker-Gard, Shelley 57
Bales, Chandra 53
Beary, Roberta 27
bending, sidney 64
Berger, Maxianne 58
Berger, David 34
Berrong, Cheryl 60
Bisshie 47
Brann, Henry 17
Budan, John 33
Burch, Susan 37
Camargo, Claire Vogel 45
Campbell, Terran 14
Carter, Terry Ann 24
Chaney, Anette 15

Cheung, Antoinette	62
Clarke, Marion	53, 69
Clifton, Daphne	45
Constable, Susan	46, 73
Constantineau, Vera	31
Cook, Priscilla	29
Deegan, Bill	45
de sousa, elehna	52
Dowis, June Rose	41
Dudley, Michael	26
Dutt, Baisali Chatterjee	19
Dutt, Gurpreet	35
Fazio, Marisa	28
Fingon, Joan C	44
Fleming, Victor	22
Forsythe, Robert	47
Freiling, Mike	50
French, Terri L	54
Garcia, Dianne	18
Gargiulo, Marita	28
Gerlits, Lisa	25
Grandstaff, Sari	17
Green, John S	21
Haggerty, Maureen Lanagan	71
Hambrick, Jennifer	18
Harrison, Carole	32
Harvey, Alan	36
Hrenchuk, Charlotte	26
Hutchison, Connie	53

Iyer, Lakshmi	35
Jambor, Lynne	22
Judkins, Carol	13
Kane, Emily W.	65
Kelsey, Julie Bloss	37
kjmunro	49
Klacsanzky, Nicholas	67
Kolodji, Deborah P.	50
Lawlor, Noreen	57
Lee, Michael Henry	49
Lehmann, Kat	33
Lindquist, Kristen	21
LoRe, Josephine	63
Louann, Franci	19
Lukstein, Janis Albright	37
Lysenko, Myron	46
MacRury, Carole	31
Mahoney, Dorothy	40, 68
Makino, Annette	13
Manley, C. R.	24
Marc, Shirley	51
Martin, Seretta	17
Matthews, Dorothy Avery	42
McCullough, Vicki	48
McDonald, Tanya	7, 58
Metzler, Sarah	48, 69, 70
Monk, Aleksandra	51
mori, isabella	27
Moss, Ron C.	14

Mumford, Leanne 49
Newcomer, MJ 38
Notarnicola, Wendy Toth 42
Ogden, Helen 30
Padden, Lorraine A. 38, 68
Painting, Tom 29
Palley, Robin 36, 73
Paris, Sarah 55
Parvez, Firdaus 25
Pearce, Jacquie 73
Phillips, Pippa 59, 72
Pillai, Madhuri 30
Pirie, Pearl 41
Poquoc, Claudia 54
Powell, Marilyn 59
pruett, m. shane 55
Quindt, Laura 29
Radmore, Claudia Coutu 60
Rajkumar, Milan 43
Ramesh, Kala 26
Redmond, Bob 50
Rehling, Mike 22, 71
Roberts, Joan Marie 63
Roman, Jonathan 20
Rosenow, Ce 33
Salzer, Jacob 34
Santos, Bona M. 38
Sauvage, Kelly 61
Schaefer, Michelle 21

Shrode, Judt	56
Singh, Kashiana	61
Sondik, Sheila	54
spooner, susan	56, 70
St-Laurent, Sandra	62
Sterba, Carmen	57
Stevens, Mary	44
Swanson, R. J.	34
Tashiro, Cathy	39
Terry, Angela	62
Tice, Kathleen I.	16
Tice, Richard	39
Villa, Christine L.	61, 72
Wakimoto, Patricia	32
Wallihan, Diane	30
Wanderer, Alice	16
Watts, Lew	23
Weers, Kim	58, 70
Welch, Michael Dylan	41
Wenk-Harrison, Christine	20
Wiggerman, Scott	15
Wilson, Garry	43
Wilson, Kath Abela	25
Wynand, Genevieve	18
Yee, Sharon Lynne	46
Young, Sharon	40

www.ingramcontent.com/pod-product-compliance
Lightning Source LLC
Chambersburg PA
CBHW020958090426
42736CB00010B/1367